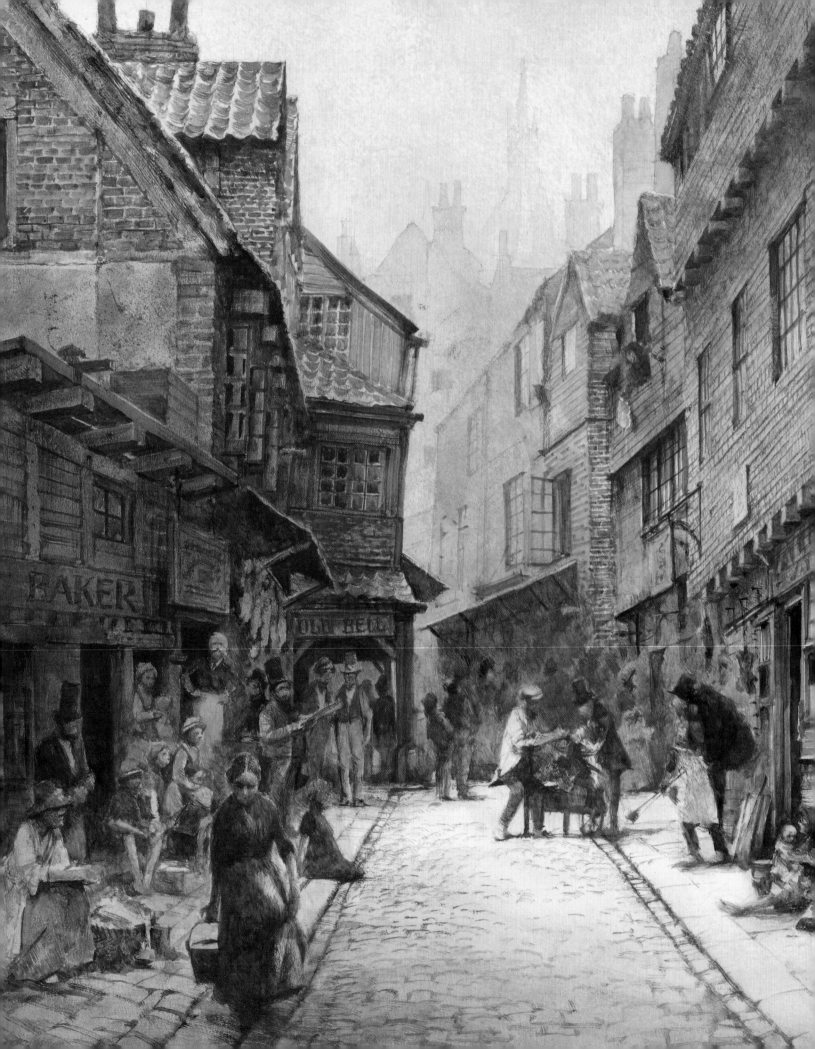

DICKENS

HIS WORK AND HIS WORLD

MICHAEL ROSEN

~ *illustrated by* ~

ROBERT INGPEN

CANDLEWICK PRESS
CAMBRIDGE, MASSACHUSETTS

For my father, who read us the whole of **Great Expectations**
and **Little Dorrit** *in a tent at night, the books lit by nothing*
more than a hurricane lamp ~ with all the voices an' all!

M. R.

First U.S. paperback edition 2008

The Library of Congress has cataloged the hardcover edition as follows:

Rosen, Michael, date.
Dickens : his work and his world / Michael Rosen ; illustrated by Robert Ingpen.
p.   cm.
Includes bibliographic references and index.
ISBN 978-0-7636-2752-2 (hardcover)
1. Dickens, Charles, 1812–1870—Juvenile literature.
2. Novelists, English—19th century—Biography—Juvenile literature.   I. Ingpen, Robert R. II. Title.
PR4581.R67 2005
823'.8—dc22   [B]   2004061847
ISBN 978-0-7636-3888-7 (paperback)

10 9 8 7 6 5 4 3 2 1

Printed in China

This book was typeset in Bernhard Modern and Locarno Italic.
The illustrations were done in watercolor.

Candlewick Press
2067 Massachusetts Avenue
Cambridge, Massachusetts 02140

visit us at www.candlewick.com

Contents

CHAPTER ONE

The Tour

A MAN with a beard, his hair thinning on top but bushy at the sides, stands on a stage. He is performing in a hall in Washington, D.C. In the audience is the president of the United States, Andrew Johnson. There are some books on a little table to one side, but the man doing the show doesn't have to look at them—he knows all the words. He is acting out stories, famous stories that he himself has written, stories that have been read by millions of people. This one-man show that he's doing is one he's put on many times before—all over England, Ireland, and the United States.

One moment he acts out one character; the next he changes his voice and becomes someone else. So one second he's Scrooge, the mean old miser from *A Christmas Carol*. "Will you not speak to me?" he cries out to a ghost. It's the Ghost of Christmas Yet To Come. The man's face looks anxious, and the audience watches in breathless silence. Later he becomes someone named Mrs. Cratchit, smiling proudly, bringing in a pudding for her family, and the audience erupts into cheers. Then he plays her husband, Bob Cratchit, crying over the death of their son Tiny Tim, and moans, "My little, little child! My little child!" The audience falls into painful silence.

This was Charles Dickens the actor, re-creating scenes from a book he had written. He was very good at playing to his audience's feelings, so when one of his characters says, "It's your Uncle Scro-o-o-o-oge!" he would draw the word out in a blood-curdling way. An American writer noticed the way he was comical one moment, savage the next. He could make his face long, give his eyes a twinkle, or roll them about, lifting his eyebrows. When he read the brutal death of Nancy in *Oliver Twist*, he acted out Bill Sikes beating her with a club, as well as Nancy's terrible struggles. Audiences were thrilled. Dickens wrote: "I should think we had . . . a dozen to twenty ladies taken out stiff and rigid."

As you can imagine, Dickens's performances exhausted him. In April 1868, while he was in the United States, he collapsed and had to cancel the rest of the tour. He came home to England, but the following January he was back on the London stage. Now, though, he had trouble pronouncing the names of the characters in his books. He was calling Pickwick "Picnic" or even "Peckwicks." It brought tears to people's eyes and made Dickens cry too as he came out to thank his audience at the end of his very last show in March 1870. Here he was, only fifty-eight years old, physically and mentally a wreck.

"From these garish lights," he said, his voice shaking, "I vanish now for evermore, with a heartfelt, grateful, respectful, affectionate farewell." He left the stage, but the clapping and cheering wouldn't stop. The audience didn't want to say goodbye, and so he came back on, his face wet with tears. He kissed his hand, turned, and was never seen in public again.

Dickens died three months later, on June 9. He was buried in Poets' Corner in London's Westminster Abbey, a final resting place for the best-known and best-loved writers. For two days, thousands of mourners filed past, throwing flowers on the coffin until the open grave was filled to overflowing. It's said that a market girl in Drury Lane who heard that Dickens had died said, "Dickens dead? Then will Father Christmas die too?"

But in a way, Dickens hasn't died. Far from it. If possible, his stories have become even more popular. They've been turned into

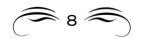

plays, films, cartoons, musicals, and TV dramas and have been seen all over the world. His characters appear in ads, on postage stamps, and on Christmas cards. Listening to a conversation, you might hear a strange phrase like "Bah! Humbug!" or people talking about peculiar places like a rag-and-bone shop or wonderfully strange-sounding characters like the Artful Dodger, Uriah Heep, Abel Magwitch, Mr. Podsnap, Mr. Bumble, Wackford Squeers, Mrs. Gamp, and Mr. Gradgrind. There's even a word—*Dickensian*—

that comes from Charles Dickens's name. So—a special word, famous characters, sayings, and places. Who are these people, where are these strange places, and why do we so like remembering them?

That's what we're going to find out in this book.

CHAPTER TWO

∼ The Life ∼

GREAT writers aren't often people born into some special family, nor are they necessarily very rich or very clever or very lucky. They're not always people who have seen or heard hundreds of amazing or odd things. But a great writer has to be someone who spends a good deal of time watching, listening, and wondering—and a good deal more time telling us about it.

When Charles John Huffam Dickens was born, he found himself in a small first-floor bedroom at the front of a little house in Portsmouth, on the south coast of England. It was Friday, February 7, 1812, and baby Charles had an eighteen-month-old sister, Frances, or Fanny, as she was called. The view from the window of the bedroom was (and still is!) of a small front garden, but in those days, you could also see fields of hay and vegetables, some windmills, and beyond them, Portsmouth Harbour. The room had no carpets, just bare boards, and at night it was lit with oil lamps and candles.

Charles's mother, who was twenty-three when he was born, was named Elizabeth, and she came from a family of musical instrument makers. He said that she often sent his sisters and him "into uncontrollable fits of laughter by her funny sayings and inimitable mimicry"—or, as we would say now, doing impressions of other people. But there was scandal in her family: not long before Charles was born, Elizabeth's father stole some money from the Navy Pay Office, and when he was found out, he ran away to the Isle of Man.

Charles's father, John, worked for the navy. Nothing special, he was the man who helped do the sums and keep the records in the office that paid out the seamen's money. But he liked to pretend he was grander than he was. He dressed like a gentleman and spoke in an upper-class voice. Perhaps he was imitating his parents, who had been servants in upper-class people's houses. He was always, always, always short of money, and always either spending it or borrowing it.

One of the most important things about Charles's childhood was that his family never stayed very long in the same house. Five months after he was born, they moved to another street in the same town. Eighteen months later, they moved again, and the first of Charles's six younger brothers and sisters was born. Soon after that, they had to move into lodgings (what we would now call an apartment) in a house that's still there in London's West End. It wasn't long before they moved again, to a place on the east coast, Sheerness, and then to the port of Chatham. Chatham seemed a magical place to Charles, age five. A "dream of chalk, and drawbridges, and mastless ships, in a muddy river," he called it. There were tunnels and fields to play in, streets full of poor and maimed soldiers and sailors just back from the wars, and a river for outings where you could sail past boats of all shapes and sizes—even a hospital ship and prison ships—and a dockyard where ships were built.

Charles's first school was his mother. "I faintly remember her teaching me the alphabet," he said, but after that he went with his older sister, Fanny, to what was called at that time a dame school. An old lady, sitting in a room over a shop where clothes were dyed, tried to teach a small group of children how to read and write. She "ruled the world

with the birch," Dickens said, meaning a birch stick that she used to beat the children.

Very soon, young Charles began to read picture books "all about scimitars and slippers and turbans and dwarfs and giants and genii and fairies, and Blue-beards and bean-stalks and riches and caverns and forests . . . and all new and all true." He loved "Jack the Giant-Killer" and "Little Red Riding Hood." As an adult, he could still bring to mind scenes from these books: a bull pulling a bell rope in the nursery rhyme "Who Killed Cock Robin?"; a Russian peasant in the snow; a ray of light on Cain in the story from the Bible in which Cain kills Abel. "Different peculiarities of dress, of face, of gait, of manner, were written indelibly on my memory," Dickens wrote later. Verses from poems and hymns, as well as the stories that the family's servants told, went into the little boy's mind too and stayed there—along with memories of flying a kite, seeing the future king ride by in a coach, watching a man with a wooden leg, staring at a line of convicts bound together by chains, and getting into trouble for saying that some paper that looked like marble wasn't real marble!

Dickens was also haunted by one particular image: "It's a figure that I once saw, just after dark, chalked upon a door in a little back lane near a country church. . . . It horrified me. . . . It smokes a pipe, and has a big hat with each of its ears sticking out . . . a pair of goggle eyes, and hands like two bunches of carrots." Even when he was a world-famous writer, he would lie awake at night and remember "the running home, the looking behind, the horror of its following me."

Sometimes he was taken by relatives (for what was at that time a huge treat) to the theater in London. On one occasion, he saw the famous clown Grimaldi. Near his home was another theater, the Theatre Royal, Rochester, which is still standing today. Dickens called it a "sweet, dingy, shabby little country theatre." Here he saw plays by Shakespeare, like *Macbeth,* with its horror and murders, but also comedies, thrillers, and pantomimes. He loved them all, especially the pantomimes, with their moments of sadness and craziness, their comic dances and rhymed speeches, their boldness, madness, coarseness, and splendor. In those days, actors also staged extracts from their shows at fairs in the open air, and he adored these too.

At home he played with paper and cardboard theaters, controlling the characters with wires. He would put on plays and do all the voices, moving the little figures on and off the stage. It wasn't long before he was singing and reciting for parties, and even standing on the table, singing duets with his sister Fanny at the Mitre Inn in Rochester.

When he was nine, Charles left the dame school and went to a school run by the young son of a Baptist minister. Here he had to recite famous poems, learn grammar, do arithmetic and handwriting, and study the morals of the stories in the Bible. At home, though, he gave himself another kind of education—reading the books on his father's shelves, like *Robinson Crusoe* and *Gulliver's Travels*, and especially one called *Tales of the Genii*—a version of *Arabian Nights*. People who knew Dickens as a boy said he used to go up to the top of the house while the other children were out playing, and pore over books and act out the characters to the audience of furniture in the room. "In all these golden fables," he said later, "there was never gold enough for me. I always wanted more. I saw no reason why there should not be mountains and rivers of gold, instead of paltry little caverns and olive pots." At another time he said he used to get his revenge on people he disliked by turning them into the bad characters in the books.

So here we see Charles, ten years old, engrossed in books, and then all on his own, acting them out, turning real life into stories, real people into characters in his little plays. But he was often miserable. Some kind of illness, which people today think was connected with his kidneys, slowed him down all through his childhood. It meant he often had to lie and watch others play rather than join them. A brother and a sister died because of illness, so the danger and worry of poor health and the terrible sadness of a child's death were never far from his family's thoughts.

Times at home were far from easy. John and Elizabeth Dickens went on having children, but John spent more money than he earned. This meant that when Charles was ten, the family had to pack up and move to what was then the edge of London, Camden Town. This wasn't the desperately poor, cramped, slum London that appears in many of Dickens's books. It was more like a village, with fields and footpaths, no streetlights or buses. Even so, Dickens remembered it as dingy, damp, and dismal, and their house as having a wretched little back garden. His father became increasingly ill-tempered and seemed less interested in him—or so Dickens would say later in life.

Although Charles loved school, his father made him stop going, as they couldn't afford it, and yet he paid for Charles's older sister, Fanny, to go to the Royal Academy of Music in 1823, where she studied piano, grammar, religious education, arithmetic, and Italian. Charles felt hurt and abandoned. Fanny had been his great friend at school, and now here she was, leaving him. Perhaps he even felt that Fanny was cheating him of what he wanted or should by rights have for himself.

It was at this time that Charles, young as he was, started wandering the streets of London by himself. He would also go with the rest of the family to visit relatives in the industrial parts of London and down by the River Thames. This wasn't just a matter of sightseeing, although the rows of houses, the masts of ships rising above the rooftops, the boat building, and the chain making all made a strong impression on Dickens. The visits were often a form of begging. His father would go to see relatives and friends to ask them for money, and Charles would find himself taking part in scenes that crop up over and over again in his books: poor people trying to make a living, people who were once well off now ruined, better-off people talking to the not-so-well-off.

As the family's money situation worsened, Charles also took part in visits to the pawnbroker's. A pawnbroker is someone who will give you some money for things you own. A short while later, if you can't buy them back, he will sell them. What this meant to Charles was that all the things in his house that he loved and cared about might sometime soon be sitting in a shop window. Even cutlery, books, chairs, and silk hankies might fetch a few pennies, but their loss made the Dickens family home poorer and poorer.

All this was bad enough, but what happened next was even worse. Just after his twelfth birthday, Charles was sent to work at Warren's Blacking—a factory where they made black boot polish. It was right by the muddy, stinking River Thames, "a crazy, tumble-down old house" with "rotten floors and staircase, and the old grey rats swarming down in the cellars, and the sound of their squeaking and scuffling coming up the stairs at all times." It was a place that would appear in one shape or another in many of Dickens's books.

Charles's job was to take a pot full of blacking and cover it first with oily paper, then with blue paper, tie it round with string, and cut the paper close to the string so that it looked neat. Next he had to paste a printed label onto each pot. He walked three miles to the factory, worked for ten and a half hours a day, with just a lunch break at twelve and a tea break in the late afternoon, and then walked the three miles home. As you read this, you might try to imagine doing this yourself, age twelve, for six days a week, month after month. You can see why people say that Charles Dickens had his childhood "snatched from him."

A few days after Charles started work at Warren's Blacking, his father was arrested for debt and sent to a special prison for people who owed money. This meant that the family was broken up. A new scene now appeared in the young boy's life: regular visits to a cold, damp, filthy prison to see his father. Again, try to imagine how strange and difficult this must have been for him. He felt shock and horror at what had happened, but there was also the shame of falling as low as this. And he couldn't help blaming his parents, a feeling made worse when his mother went to stay with his father in prison and he was sent to lodge with a woman who lived round the corner.

At Warren's Blacking, Charles's workmates were a mix of orphans and working people's sons. We know from what he said later that he saw himself as superior to these boys and that being with them felt like a humiliation. Yet they were kind to him. When he fell to the floor with one of the seizures that his illness brought on, his workmates laid him on the straw on the factory floor, filled some empty blacking pots with hot water, and put them next to his body, close to where the pain was. Charles became friendly with one boy in particular, Bob Fagin, and he was to use his name much later in *Oliver Twist*.

There were some pleasures. His mother would sometimes come and see him at Warren's. He played on the coal barges with his workmates during their breaks. Best of all, though, was the money he earned. The one good thing about his father being bankrupt and in prison was that part of the money Charles got from Warren's was his own to spend. He carefully counted it out into little piles, and whenever he could, he would visit grand eating places, like a beef house on Drury Lane, a tavern on Parliament Street, or a coffee shop in the West End. He would order a meal and a drink, tip the waiter, and stroll back to his room.

It was at this time that Dickens started doing what he would do for the rest of his life: he told stories to the people around him. Some were straight fibs—about how he lived in this or that grand house. They helped mark him out as different, a young gentleman almost, even though the Dickens family was down at the bottom of society. But any dreams he might have had of being as grand as the people in the books he had read were now dashed. He had fallen into what people today call the poverty trap, a place it looks as if you can never get out of. And it depressed and terrified him.

John Dickens didn't stay in prison, even though the memory of it would remain in Charles's mind. When he was released, he went back to work, and father and son would walk the three miles together down from the suburbs into the city, joining long lines of clerks, office boys, factory workers, servants, and errand boys. And, as the world knows, Charles Dickens didn't spend the rest of his life slaving away in factories, though most of the people he worked with at that time did.

His father found a way for him to get back to his education. In 1825 Charles started at Wellington House Academy, a school—but not one you would recognize. In one big room, two hundred boys sat

on benches laid out in rows. Everything that was taught was learned by heart, often chanted. Older boys had to make sure that the younger children got everything right. Much of the writing was done on small black stone slabs called slates. If paper was used, the writing was done with a sharpened feather called a quill. Mistakes, rudeness, and naughtiness were punished with beatings.

Though Dickens would later write about schools as if they weren't much better than prisons, and about schoolteachers as if they weren't much better than torturers, it seems that at Wellington House, Charles and some of his friends formed a club. They wrote and put on plays, recited poems and songs, wrote stories, put them into scrapbooks, and produced a magazine called *Our Newspaper*. They loaned it to other boys to read and were paid in marbles or pencils. Here's one of their jokes: "Lost. By a boy with a long red nose, and grey eyes, a very bad temper. Whoever has found the same may keep it, as the owner is better without it."

School lasted for only two years, as the family hit yet more money problems, and at the age of fifteen, Charles Dickens was sent out to work again, this time for a lawyer. He was what we would call today an office boy. Long before typewriters, photocopiers, and computers, he spent the day copying out papers by hand. He would also act as a runner or gofer, carrying lawyers' files and documents from one office to another or to clients' houses. The work itself was often dull, but the offices were full of

characters from all walks of life, and it wasn't long before Dickens got a
name for himself as the lad who could imitate people—the old laundry
lady who sniffed powdered tobacco (called snuff), for instance. In the
evenings—every evening—Charles went to the theater. This fed into his
acts so that, when asked, he could recite a bit of Shakespeare or sing a
popular song. Theaters at this time weren't fancy or just for the upper
classes. They were riotous, drunken, dirty, often violent places where every
kind of illegal trade was happening. Dickens loved them!

While he worked for the lawyers, the teenage Charles decided to do a little extra skills training. He taught himself shorthand—writing down exactly what someone says in a quick code so that it can later be translated into proper English. Anyone who reads a Dickens book is immediately struck by the way people speak. The dialogue sounds real, and different people talk with different accents and mannerisms. Some of this can be put down to the fact that Charles was a brilliant mimic and actor, but we should also remember that he learned how to write as fast as people spoke.

It was this skill that led him to his next job. At the age of eighteen, he advertised himself as a "shorthand writer," and it wasn't long before he was sitting in law courts, scribbling away. Soon after, he took on the same job in Parliament, writing down speeches as the politicians debated the great issues of the day. And he also turned what he saw into sketches—accounts of what he heard and what he thought of it. The newspaper he wrote for was what we might call liberal or left-wing today, though what it campaigned for we take for granted: votes for all, freedom of speech, and the end of rule by lords and dukes—in other words, reform. In Dickens's day these were ideas that hadn't been accepted, and he placed himself firmly on the side of the reformers.

In his spare time, he wrote little plays, and his moments of real pleasure came in arranging family gatherings with shows, music, and recitations. Fanny, having spent some time at the Royal Academy of

Music, could be relied on to produce some good singing and piano playing. But this kind of fun and games is a long way from the stories that he would later write. So when did he begin to come up with the kind of writing that would lead to his great novels?

In 1833, at the age of twenty-one, he wrote a short piece called "A Dinner at Poplar Walk." It's a comic story of a family trying to chase money that they think they're owed from dead relatives—not hard to imagine what might have inspired that! "With fear and trembling," Dickens dropped it into the "dark letter-box in a dark office" of the *Monthly Magazine*. He didn't hear from them, but when he went to buy the next issue, printed for all to read was "A Dinner at Poplar Walk." As he walked down to Westminster, his eyes were "so dimmed with joy and pride" that he could hardly stand looking at the street or the reality of the world around him.

Over the next few months, he wrote eight more stories, all published, none of which earned him any money. They were all humorous, often poking fun at the people who inhabited the same walk of life as his own family—the lower-middle class.

The next step for Dickens was working for a much better, bigger paper than the *Monthly Magazine*—the famous *Morning Chronicle*. He was its parliamentary sketch writer but also a theater reviewer and reporter on election campaigns, dinners, public meetings, and the like. This meant traveling all over the country, writing enormous amounts at great speed about things almost as they happened. For the first time, he saw life all over England: life on the road, life in the industrial north. Soon he was writing other kinds of articles: comic, witty, or punchy commentaries on topical subjects. He was the forerunner of the columnist in today's newspapers. But even as he was rushing into this new venture, his father was in trouble again. And as the law was preparing to cart John Dickens back off to prison, Charles was writing stories full of descriptions of debtors' lockups.

He was building quite a reputation for conjuring up in his articles the London he saw and heard. Snatches of conversation appeared alongside descriptions of the poor, the rich, the crowds, the pleasure gardens, the fairs, the slum tenements. In 1836 all these articles and sketches were published in a book, *Sketches by Boz*, with pictures by the most famous illustrator of the day, George Cruikshank. Charles Dickens was beginning to make his mark.

What happened next, though, was a piece of work that would change the way stories were written. Dickens produced a monthly tale about a group of friends. Each month, people could buy the next installment for a shilling, building it into a full-length novel. This was the beginning of what came to be his main method of writing, and one of the most exciting things about his work: the chapter-by-chapter unfolding of events, each chapter leading up to a cliffhanger. It was the beginning of a kind of storytelling we are all familiar with today: the serial, the soap opera that develops day by day or week by week, a tale with many characters whose fortunes rise and fall alongside one another. Dickens's book was called *The Pickwick Papers*.

Dickens would spend the next thirty years or so writing, editing, and performing. In 1836 he married Catherine Hogarth, the daughter of his employer at the *Morning Chronicle*'s sister paper, the *Evening Chronicle*. In the years that followed, he became the father of ten children. Later in life, however, Dickens fell in love with another woman, and he separated from his wife in 1858. He died at the age of fifty-eight, in 1870.

"*Fog everywhere*. Fog up the river, where it flows among green aits and meadows; fog down the river, where it rolls defiled among the tiers of shipping, and the waterside pollutions of a great (and dirty) city. Fog on the Essex Marshes, fog on the Kentish heights. Fog creeping into the cabooses of collier-brigs; fog lying out on the yards, and hovering in the rigging of great ships; fog drooping on the gunwales of barges and small boats. Fog in the eyes and throats of ancient Greenwich pensioners, wheezing by the firesides of their wards; fog in the stem and bowl of the afternoon pipe of the wrathful skipper, down in his close cabin; fog cruelly pinching the toes and fingers of his shivering little 'prentice boy on deck.

Chance people on the bridges peeping over the parapets into a nether sky of fog, with fog all round them, as if they were up in a balloon, and hanging in the misty clouds."

from

BLEAK HOUSE

CHAPTER THREE

London

EVERYONE lives in a particular time and place. But how does the time and place we live in affect us?

If you stop to think about yourself and wonder why you are the way you are, you'll realize that all sorts of things make up the person who is you. First of all, there are the people who've brought you up, who've been with you perhaps since you were born—talking to you, looking after you, sometimes telling you off, and mostly, I hope, trying to be good to you. Their behavior and outlook have had a huge effect on how you think and feel.

What's more, they've set your standard of living. The money they earn has given you the home you live in, the food you eat, the outings and trips you go on, and the clubs you belong to. Often people's outlooks are influenced by the amount of money they have and the way they earn it. Someone who works sixteen hours a day, seven days a week, probably has a very different way of looking at the world from someone who never has to work because he was born rich. If someone spends all day looking after people, she might well have different views on the world from someone who works alone running her own business.

And what of the area you live in? Particular regions, localities, and whole countries have particular customs and traditions. People from the same area talk with a similar accent and language, find the same jokes funny, and share similar memories.

And what of the era you live in? Sometimes people talk about the sixties or the nineties, meaning that what happened then had a special feeling about it. Maybe these were times when a lot changed and new things started to happen, so what people lived through *then* altered the way they are *now*.

All in all, we can say that people are greatly affected by their backgrounds (their parents and family), by how and where they live, how they and their parents earn their living, and by the times they live through.

So what was England like in Charles Dickens's lifetime? And more specifically, what was London like? If I had to use one word to sum it up, I'd say *change*. In 1800, twelve years before Dickens was born, there were a million people living and working in London. By the time he was thirty-eight, there were more than two million. In fifty years, the population had doubled. The city was sucking in hundreds of thousands of people from the countryside, looking for work, and rows and rows of tiny houses, alleys, and streets were springing up every day. It was a massive upheaval.

In 1829 the illustrator George Cruikshank, whom Dickens worked with, drew a cartoon called *London Going Out of Town, or The March of*

Bricks and Mortar. In it, an army of robots made of spades, chimney pots, and troughs of cement carries a placard saying:

This GROUND to be Lett or a Building Lease.
Enquire of Mr. Goth,
Brick Maker, Bricklayers Arms,
Brick Lane, Brixton.

(He's called Mr. Goth because it was the Goths who destroyed Rome in Roman times.) The robot army is marching on fields full of trees and haystacks, which are crying out, "Oh I am mortally wounded" and "Our fences I fear will be found to be no defence against these Barbarians. . . ." "I must leave the field," wails a tree as the robot army comes nearer. A brick-making kiln is firing a great arch of bricks into the air and onto a haystack, while the sky is full of smoke belching out of the chimneys of houses and factories.

Into the middle of all this change, and as part of it, came the railways. Between 1837 and 1863, almost all of London's mainline stations (most of which are still standing today) were built. This meant that it became possible for people with money to travel around Britain much more quickly and easily. Interestingly enough, although Dickens was a great traveler himself, using every modern means available, in his books people more often than not travel by the old ways. Perhaps he was trying to capture a sense of what the world was like just before the change.

And what were all the people who came to live in London doing? We can start with Dickens and his family. John Dickens came where the work was and had to stay when he got into debt. He worked, you'll remember, as a clerk—someone who spent all day with a pen in his hand, filling in figures—and Charles too began work as a copy-clerk, writing out documents. London was conducting business with people all over the country and throughout the British Empire. Business needs paper, documents, and files, and before the days of computers, this meant thousands of people writing and looking after all those bits of paper. So London became the first place in the world that had a large army of clerks working for every kind of business—shops, law firms, and government and local councils.

As we know, John Dickens went to prison because he couldn't pay his debts. But there were other kinds of poor people in London. This was a time long before you could collect benefits if you didn't have a job. If you couldn't find work, you had to beg, borrow, steal, or starve—or, in some situations, go to the workhouse, a kind of part boarding house, part prison, part labor camp where very poor people were put. There you would have to do work like breaking stones or stripping rope. You might not be able to get

a job because you were ill, old, pregnant, injured from war wounds, or born disabled, but it might also be because your business or trade was failing and there was no work for people like you. In London, in Dickens's lifetime, this meant there was an army of the desperately poor, sleeping out in the streets or crammed eight to ten to a room in the shacks and tenements on the east side of the city and along the river.

Between the clerks and the destitute (as these desperately poor people were called) were people who did manual work in the hundreds of factories that were springing up all over the city. And another kind of work also helped swell London's population—domestic labor. People with any money to spare, after they had paid the rent and bought food, would have servants. Even the Dickens household, often on the verge of ruin, kept servants. So that was another army! An army of servants, errand boys, live-in maids, nannies and nurses, cooks and kitchen maids, boys who looked after the horses, and so on. Often living in their masters' and mistresses' houses, many of these workers were paid next to nothing and had to do whatever they were told. They weren't allowed to marry or see whomever they wanted, and were thrown out when they became ill or too old or if the family didn't like them. It was intimate work—if you were a servant, you would get to know the people you worked for extremely well. Dickens's writing often looks very closely at people in service and how they were treated.

I've said that London "sucked in" hundreds of thousands of people. Where did they come from? Mostly they came from small towns, villages, and hamlets all over England, as well as from Ireland and from places across the British Empire, including Africa, India, and the Caribbean. This meant that many of the people in London had lived through the experience of moving there. It wasn't just a matter of travel, but of upheaval, of putting aside one way of life and adopting

another. The mind of someone who had made this kind of move would be full of contrasts: "I used to do this; now I do that. My street used to look like that; now it looks like this."

It was something that Dickens himself experienced, and it figures in his books.

With all these developments—and because of them—came big changes in people's expectations. Dickens lived through a time that bubbled with ideas about new ways to run things. Not long before he was born, two big events sent great waves through Britain: the French and American revolutions. These weren't only a question of wars and executions but also of what are called rights. Dickens grew up in and lived through a time when many questions were being asked. Here are some of them: If I am born a lord or a duke, do I have more rights than someone who isn't? Can I run my neighborhood, even run the country, simply because of what family I was born into? Or are all men born equal? If that is the case, should all men have the right to vote? Even poor men? Are women equal to men? If people *are* born equal, why are some rich and some poor? Is it because of schools and education? Are poor children taught differently from rich children? And if people are equal, does that mean everyone has the right to say and believe whatever they want? Even people who aren't Christians? When we say that everyone is equal, does that include people with dark skins? Does that mean slaves should be freed? (Dickens certainly thought so.)

But people didn't just *ask* these kinds of questions. They set up clubs, associations, and organizations. They wrote books and printed posters and leaflets. They had meetings and marches. Sometimes there were rebellions. Wherever Dickens went in the country, especially in the 1840s, when he was in his thirties, there was talk as never before about the question of rights for all. People wondered whether there would be a revolution in Britain as there had been in France and America. Indeed,

in 1848 the Chartists, a group of working people who wanted the most change, marched on London. They were protesting about voting: they wanted votes for all, votes for Parliament every year, and so on. But they were also angry because some people were incredibly rich while so many were desperately poor. Surely there had to be better—and fairer—ways of sharing things out?

These arguments were going on as Dickens was writing. It's important to realize that his books, which show so cleverly and brilliantly how people lived and what their feelings were, were a way of joining in with the great debates of the day. They are, if you like, contributions to the talk, argument, and demand for change. But when we read them, it's not easy to say that this or that book shows he definitely believed this or that—though after he wrote *Hard Times,* in 1854, it was criticized as being full of "sullen socialism." What we *do* know is that he called for the end to government by lords and dukes and was in favor of more votes for more people. He hated the way the poor were humiliated in the workhouses and the way poor children were taught in schools. The kinds of crime and misery that go hand in hand with terrible poverty seem to have made him very angry, but, also, quite literally, scared him.

As a young man sitting up in the gallery of the Houses of Parliament and jotting down the exact words that the politicians spoke, then rushing round the country hearing what they said at election time, Dickens certainly knew how they saw things, but mostly he chose not to write about them in his stories. He was more interested in showing how what politicians said and did affected the lives of ordinary people. If Parliament thought workhouses and orphanages were a good idea, Dickens says in his stories, "Well, this is what they're like. This is how bad they are." If, as some writers were saying, every man should make his own way in life, doing all he can to climb the ladder of society, Dickens asks in his books, "What happens if it wrecks his personality and ruins his soul?"

But of course, asking questions is not the same as making up stories. You have to create characters, situations, scenes. Events have to happen; good and bad things have to come out of people's thoughts and actions. As we've seen, Dickens's own life gave him a rich flow of people and situations, but writers often need a nudge to help them turn what they see, feel, and hear into stories. Quite often they need to read or see some other kind of writing that makes them think, I could do it like that! I could write about the things I want to write about in that kind of way. What was it for Dickens? Well, for one thing, he lived at a time when London had started to talk about itself—in songs, magazines, and shows at the theater, and in little stories called chapbooks that were sold on the street.

Dickens loved reading about the amazing coincidences, terrible crimes, and evil goings-on of the criminal classes, the tragic downfall of this or that person, the wicked ways of Mr. Such-and-Such, the highly peculiar behavior of Mrs. Whatsit.

He saw how much the working people around him loved reading these stories too, and so, for most of his life, his own stories appeared as serials, week by week or month by month, in popular magazines. We call him a novelist and put him in the same group as people who write a book and publish it to be read by a relatively small number of educated men and women, yet really he was part of the world of magazines and chapbooks. Because his stories were so good, they did become books, and it was Dickens more than any other writer who turned books into things that anyone who knew how to read felt happy to read. Books were no longer just for people cleverer or richer than you.

So Dickens was a man of his time; he became who he was through living and taking part in everything going on around him. But he was also one of the very few people who did something big and important to help change the world. You live in an era when you can go to a library or a shop or surf the Net and read almost anything you want. On TV and radio, people are talking nonstop about the ways of the world. Films, plays, soaps, and serials tell us stories about the way we are, the way we were, the way we could be, the way it would be awful to be, and so on. The world wasn't always like that. For hundreds of years, most people knew or had access to only the stories that came with their religion, the stories they told each other about their own lives, and what we call folk stories. Charles Dickens did as much to get us from living like that to the way we live now as any other single person.

JO THE CROSSING SWEEPER

From BLEAK HOUSE

CHAPTER FOUR

The Work

IF you were living in England in the thirty-four years between 1836 and 1870, nearly every year you could look forward to buying a magazine that would have a new piece of writing from Charles Dickens in it. A story would start, and each issue you could read what came next. Then there would be a whole month of waiting to see how things turned out for the characters, a whole month to talk to your friends and family about what might happen next. You've probably noticed that in soaps on TV, each episode usually ends with something that makes us wonder what will happen next, something that makes us want to hurry home and watch the following episode. Dickens wrote like this and has, in a way, taught the rest of the world's writers how to do it too. There is a famous story of crowds gathering on the wharves in New York, waiting for the arrival of a magazine to find out if Little Nell, in *The Old Curiosity Shop,* had died.

I'm now going to look at four of Dickens's works: *A Christmas Carol, Oliver Twist, David Copperfield,* and *Great Expectations.* He wrote fifteen novels and countless short stories, but these are four I thought you might like. I'll be telling you the plot of the first three, but with the fourth, *Great Expectations,* I'll look in greater detail at how Dickens entices his readers into his stories.

A Christmas Carol

came out December 1843

A CHRISTMAS CAROL is known all around the world. That's partly because Walt Disney made a cartoon based on the story, but there are hundreds of other plays, films, TV dramas, comic books, and so on.

Ebenezer Scrooge is a miser, someone who hoards money and detests spending it. That's why he hates Christmas, a time when you're supposed to give presents. "Every idiot who goes about with 'Merry Christmas' on his lips," he says, "should be boiled with his own pudding, and buried with a stake of holly through his heart." On Christmas Eve the ghost of Jacob Marley, his old partner in business, visits him, followed by the ghosts of Christmas Past, Christmas Present, and Christmas Yet To Come. Scrooge is shown that no one will be sorry when he dies, because he is so mean. As a result, when he wakes up on Christmas Day, he's a changed man. Instead of being the old miser everyone knows, he sends a turkey to his clerk, Bob Cratchit, starts giving money to charity, and becomes a jolly old fellow.

Perhaps you know the story so well, it's not much more than a bit of fun for you, and the way it all works out so nicey-nicey can seem a bit slushy. But behind that, some interesting things are going on. Reading the book makes us ask what the point is of going through life being

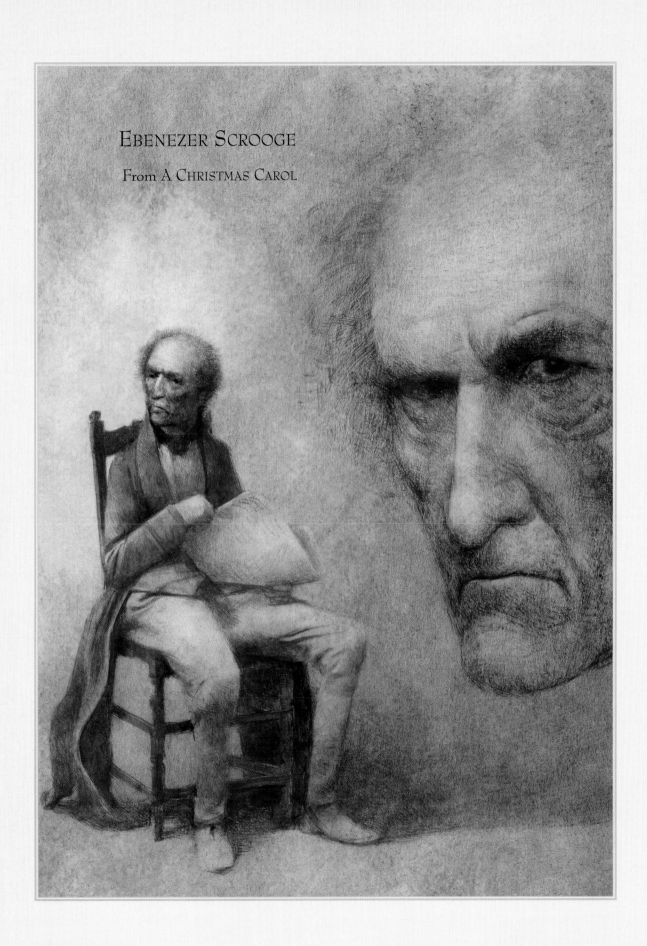

EBENEZER SCROOGE

From A Christmas Carol

mean and miserable. Is it right that a boss should pay a worker so little, just to get rich? Who in the book knows how to have a really good time? Often in the past, poor people have been shown getting drunk, spending their money when they should be saving it, and being generally ignorant. It's interesting that Scrooge, the rich person in this book, has something very important to learn from the poor.

Oliver Twist

came out monthly between January 1837 and March 1839

OLIVER TWIST is the name of a boy. He's an orphan who's being brought up in a workhouse. This means that he is treated terribly and cruelly, especially by a man called Bumble, who runs the workhouse. It's while he's there that one of the most famous scenes in English literature happens: Oliver dares to ask for more food!

Life is so horrible for him that he runs away to London, but here he falls in with a gang of boy thieves led by a man called Fagin. In the gang is a burglar called Bill Sikes; his girlfriend, Nancy; and a pickpocket known as the Artful Dodger.

This part of the book is full of adventures, and we wonder if Oliver will stay with the gang or escape from a life of crime. A man called Monks

BILL SIKES & OLIVER

From OLIVER TWIST

appears on the scene, and he seems very interested in keeping Oliver thieving. The point is that Monks knows Oliver's real background. How this comes out and who tells what to whom is both exciting and terrible because it leads eventually to Bill Sikes's murdering Nancy.

Oliver Twist opened many people's eyes to just how horrible life in a workhouse was, especially for children. In it Dickens gave these pauper children, as they're called, a voice, which was important because there was at the time no way, like film or TV, in which such children could tell the world the story of their lives.

Oliver Twist also shows child crime, which was, in a way, a dangerous thing to do. Dickens lived at a time when plenty of people thought that such things as crime shouldn't be in books for decent, respectable people. The only way it could be, they thought, was if the author kept saying how bad the criminals were, how they would end up in hell, how they should go to church to repent, or be locked up or executed. Some people felt that *Oliver Twist* made child crime look attractive and exciting, and that worried them. But the book became incredibly popular, and, of course, many people realized that Dickens was making a link between the cruel way Oliver is treated by so-called honest, law-abiding people in the first part of the book and the fact that he ends up on the streets stealing things. The story, then, was a way of joining in the talk about what to do with the poor, and what to do about crime. And every night on television, that talk's still going on, isn't it?

David Copperfield

came out monthly between May 1849 and November 1850

DAVID COPPERFIELD is the nearest Dickens came to telling his own life story in one of his novels.

David is born in the country soon after his father dies. His mother marries again, and David's stepfather, Edward Murdstone, and his sister, Miss Murdstone, are both horrible. David is sent away to school, where we meet a horrible head teacher called Creakle. David makes friends with two boys, Steerforth and Traddles. Steerforth is arrogant and handsome, while Traddles is always in a good mood and gets on with life.

David's mother dies, and Mr. Murdstone sends David—age nine—to work in a bottle factory in London. He lodges with the Micawber family, who are always short of money yet who always seem to have a good time. But life in London is just too hard, and he runs away to his aunt Betsey in Dover. Now things feel better, and he stays in Betsey Trotwood's house with a man people call a lunatic because he says he keeps getting interrupted by the head of King Charles—who was executed in 1649!

At the next house he stays in, which belongs to a lawyer named Mr. Wickfield, David meets a girl named Agnes, the lawyer's daughter. He goes to work for another lawyer and meets up again with Steerforth. Another series of events then happens involving the Peggotty

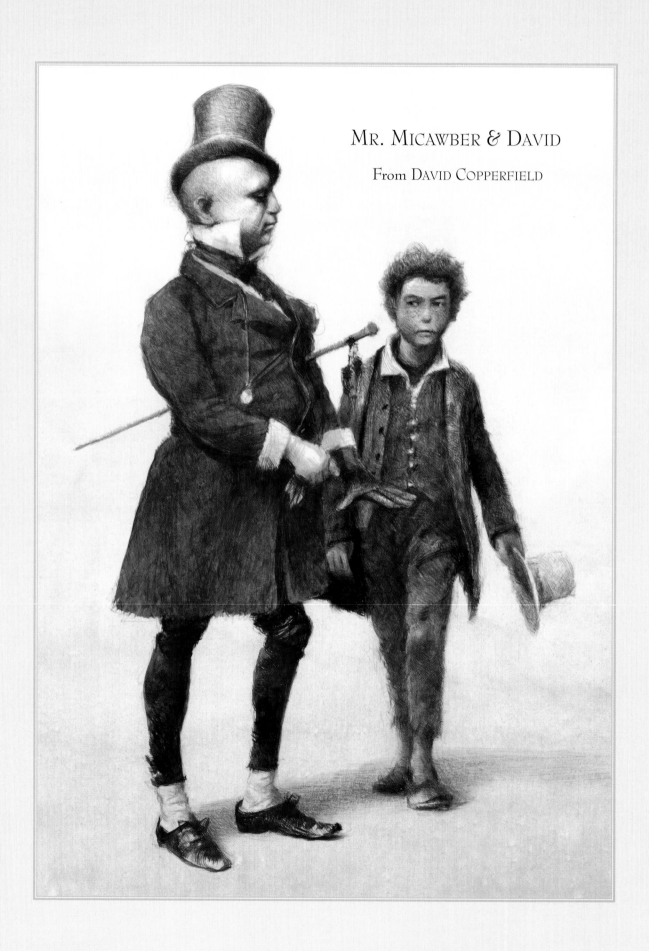

MR. MICAWBER & DAVID

From DAVID COPPERFIELD

family in Yarmouth. Steerforth gets their little girl Em'ly to break off her engagement and run away with him, and this leads to desperate unhappiness for many people until Steerforth drowns.

David marries a woman named Dora and becomes a famous writer. Dora doesn't live long, and David realizes that Agnes is the one he should have married, but by now her father, Mr. Wickfield, is being tricked by a man called Uriah Heep, who is after Agnes as well.

I won't say how it all works out in the end.

As you can see, this is a huge rambling story (or stories), more like a soap opera than the other books we've looked at. There is a constant back-and-forth among the different groups of people in the story. Cruelty and kindness sit side by side, as people secretly plot against others who have no idea what's going on. In fact, all through the book, things happen that we know about but that a character in the story doesn't. And yet we don't know how each scene is going to finish, whether the bad person will come to a sticky end or get away with it.

All this makes *David Copperfield* a gripping read. One moment we're part of a secret, seeing how this or that person is plotting against someone else, and the next we're surprised by how things turn out. It's a bit like that for David too, just as it is for us in real life.

David Copperfield is also a book that takes us from the countryside to London and back to the countryside, and it takes us traveling abroad when Em'ly's father goes looking for her. It takes us from life among the very poor to life among the well-off. It takes us deep into family loyalty and contrasts it with the way people can mistreat their stepchildren. It shows us people who live by the law and have a very strong sense of right and wrong, and others who break all the rules and don't care who they hurt. It shows us crazy people, characters who aren't crazy, and someone who is nearly driven crazy. And, at the end of the book, we see how the people of England don't live only in England. They're now going "out to the Colonies"—working and making money in the British Empire.

All this is why *David Copperfield* isn't a book only about people. It's a book about society. That means it's a book about how the different parts of a country are living. By getting us to care about what happens to people in the story, Dickens gets us to think about what is a good or a bad way to behave. He shows us how hard it is for good people to stop bad people from harming them and how easy it is not to realize what's going on.

MISS BETSEY TROTWOOD

From DAVID COPPERFIELD

Great Expectations

came out weekly between December 1860 and August 1861

IN SOME WAYS, *Great Expectations* is a bit like *David Copperfield,* as it tells the story of a boy growing into a man and trying to make his way in life.

Pip is brought up by his sister and her kind husband, Joe, a village blacksmith. He gets to know a very wealthy woman named Miss Havisham, who was deserted by her husband-to-be on the day of her wedding. She is bringing up a girl named Estella and teaching her to be cruel to men as a strange kind of revenge.

Pip starts to have ideas that he can become a "gentleman," rather than a "common labouring-boy." This is because he's told he's going to come in to some money when he's older. He assumes that it'll be coming from Miss Havisham and promptly deserts and shuns Joe, who has looked after him and loved him.

In fact, Pip has gotten a lot of things wrong—almost everything! Miss Havisham isn't the one who's left him the money, and her step-daughter, Estella, whom Pip adores and hopes to marry, treats him badly and goes off with someone else.

Great Expectations is a story that gets us thinking about what it means to turn your back on people who love you, what it means to be kind and unkind. By getting close to one person, Pip, we see how longing to turn yourself into a gentleman might easily cause you and others close to you to suffer. Interestingly, most of the people in the book who are of the "gentle," or upper-middle, class, as we might say today, are neither nice nor gentle! And because the book shows one person changing and evolving, it helps us think about whether human beings are born the way they will always be—or whether they can change.

Like all of Dickens's books, *Great Expectations* is full of stunning moments. This is partly because the person telling the story, Pip himself, has to admit over and over again that he keeps getting things wrong. This makes him an antihero—in fact, he's one of the first ever to be found in books. An antihero is someone who is the main character, the one we care about and are interested in, but instead of being clever or brave or good and right, he is weak, imperfect, often wrong, and sometimes bad. Until *Great Expectations* was published, there had been heroes who were rascals and thieves, even villains, but they were always lovable and often in some way or another a victim. What makes Pip more of an antihero is that he isn't a victim. If bad things happen to him, it's mostly his fault. The only way he becomes anything like a hero is in the way he comes to realize where he's gone wrong.

All this makes *Great Expectations* a very special book. Instead of being what we might call romantic and working out all right in the end, it shows us something more real than that. It lets us see what it feels like to be weak and not well meaning or well intentioned. It doesn't give us an easy, cozy feeling. Indeed, one of Dickens's friends was so upset that the story seemed to finish without a happy ending, he made him write a new ending in which things do look like they'll work out all right for Pip. I like to think that the first ending Dickens came up with was a better way for the book to finish. Plenty of us don't get everything right in life, and events don't always work out nice and neatly for us. Every now and then, why not have a book that runs against the tide of neat, happy endings and shows us life as it is?

As we have seen, *Great Expectations* tells the story of Pip, an orphan who is being brought up by his older sister and her husband, Joe. Mrs. Joe, as Pip calls her, is a very tough parent to her young brother. But the very first chapter shows us something even tougher. Here Dickens creates a scene that is full of terror and layered with a sense of mystery. It's part of what makes him such a powerful writer. Pip is walking in a graveyard when he is seized by someone who shouts, "Keep still, you little devil, or I'll cut your throat!" It turns out to be a convict who's escaped from a prison ship moored nearby. He's called Magwitch, and this isn't the only time in the book that he surprises us. In fact, he is the surprise of the whole book, but I don't want to give the plot away and tell you how. At this moment of terror, he wants Pip to bring him some food and a steel file, so that he can cut off the bit of chain around his leg. It's just before Pip and his family are going to have their Christmas dinner, so Pip steals some food and drink for Magwitch.

The Christmas dinner scene is agonizing as Mrs. Joe goes to serve up drink that Pip has stolen and swapped with a horrible medicine called tar-water, and then looks for a pie that he has given to Magwitch. It's agonizing partly because Mrs. Joe is very scary, but also because someone is there who is just that much richer than Pip's family.

He is Joe's uncle Pumblechook (though Mrs. Joe seems rather more fond of him than her husband). He's "a large hard-breathing middle-aged slow man, with a mouth like a fish, dull staring eyes, and sandy hair standing upright on his head, so that he looked as if he had just been all but choked." And next thing, in the story, Pumblechook does indeed choke when he drinks the tar-water! Pip only gets out of what would have been terrible trouble when soldiers capture Magwitch, who tells them that *he* stole the food and drink. Close shave! This is typical Dickens: a scene where we know more than some of the key characters. When Mrs. Joe goes out to get the drink, we know, like Pip, that it's tar-water, so we share his agony. It becomes our agony. What happens to Pip matters to us. This is what we mean when we say that a writer "engages our sympathy," and no one does it better than Dickens.

We worry that Pip will be in terrible trouble. We see that dangerous and frightening things are going on "out there," and that at home things aren't too safe either.

One day, Mrs. Joe comes back from market with Uncle Pumblechook and says to Joe, "If this boy ain't grateful this night, he never will be!" The news is that Miss Havisham, from uptown, wants Pip to go and play at her house. Pip takes up the story: "I had heard of Miss Havisham up town—everybody for miles round, had heard of Miss Havisham up town—as an immensely rich and grim lady who lived in a large and dismal house barricaded against robbers, and who led a life of seclusion." We hear that Uncle Pumblechook has recommended Pip to her. How we learn this is one of the many moments in *Great Expectations* that can best be described as uncomfortable. Mrs. Joe is not only terrifying and hard on her little brother—she is also a snob. She is a snob toward people she thinks are beneath her, and that includes her husband, a kind, loving, and utterly decent man. And she grovels toward people she thinks of as above her, like Uncle Pumblechook and Miss Havisham.

This is how she explains the situation to Joe:

"And couldn't Uncle Pumblechook, being always considerate and thoughtful for us—though you may not think it, Joseph," in a tone of the deepest reproach, as if he were the most callous of nephews, "then mention this boy, standing Prancing here"—which I solemnly declare I was not doing—"that I have for ever been a willing slave to?"

Here you see Mrs. Joe rushing through her thoughts and words, only half making sense, trying to say everything at once, and showing herself to be snobbish and groveling, and horrible to Pip all at the same time! And it's all conveyed in what someone is saying: Dickens reveals what Mrs. Joe is thinking even though she may not know what she is telling us about herself.

Going to see Miss Havisham means that Pip must be cleaned up, as Mrs. Joe says that he is "grimed with crock and dirt from the hair of his head to the sole of his foot!" ("Crock" is soot from the chimney.) He is pounced on "like an eagle on a lamb," his face "squeezed into wooden bowls in sinks," and he is "soaped, and kneaded, and towelled, and thumped, and harrowed, and rasped" until, he says, "I really was quite beside myself." He is put into clean clothes "of the stiffest character . . . trussed up" in his "tightest and fearfullest suit." (By the way, there's no such word as *fearfullest,* but Dickens loved to make up words. It was a way of making the true feelings of a character break through as if ordinary words aren't quite up to the job.) Here he is working with symbols—that's to say, what we are being shown means something else, suggests something more. Over and over again in *Great Expectations,* we see Pip struggling with his feelings of wanting to get on in life, to succeed, to better himself. So this moment of cleaning himself up is not only a matter of trying to cleanse himself of something dirty but is also symbolic of cleansing himself of his background, washing off something he's ashamed of. At this stage both Pip and we, the readers, are only dimly aware of this.

Anyway, at last Pip is ready to leave. "Boy," says Uncle Pumblechook:

"Be for ever grateful to all friends, but especially unto them which brought you up by hand!"

"Good-bye, Joe!"

"God bless you, Pip, old chap!"

You can see here the great difference between Pumblechook and his nephew, Joe, expressed entirely in what they say. The uncle always has to deliver little lessons to Pip, making him feel less than he is, while Joe simply blesses Pip. Pumblechook calls him "boy"; Joe calls him "Pip, old chap!" So in the dialogue Dickens reveals what people are like as events move on and change.

One way of looking at different people is to see them standing on different rungs of a ladder. By now in *Great Expectations,* Dickens has shown us someone on the very bottom (Abel Magwitch); someone who might be called "poor but honest" (Joe); someone who thinks she's above that (Mrs. Joe); someone who is a notch above (Uncle Pumblechook); and someone we've heard of but not seen who is much higher still (Miss Havisham). Dickens is especially good at showing people across the whole of society, bumping into each other, in conflict with each other, and moving up and down the social ladder—just as he did in his own life, and just as he saw people doing in the world around him.

Pip, as we guess by now, is the person who will be having the "great expectations" of the title. Or, to put it another way, where on the ladder will Pip end up? As he goes off in the little horse and cart, he says that he sees the stars coming out one by one, "without throwing any light on the questions why on earth I was going to play at Miss Havisham's, and what on earth I was expected to play at."

End of chapter!

Here Dickens gives us what is called a cliffhanger. We are left wanting to know what happens next and wondering if there is more going on than meets the eye. This sense of mystery and tension is Dickens's powerful way of telling us that life is full of secrets just waiting to unravel, and in unraveling, they change who we think we are. As we sit there after a cliffhanger, we are left thinking, Oh, so that's how it is. Well, that changes things, doesn't it? *Now* what's going to happen?

Chapter Eight of *Great Expectations* is one of the most amazing chapters in literature.

We begin at Uncle Pumblechook's house, with him quizzing Pip on his sums in a domineering way. "Seven times nine, boy?" he asks pompously. And all through breakfast, Pumblechook keeps it up: "And four?" "And eight?" "And six?" "And two?" "And ten?"

Here's Dickens creating comedy in a situation in which one person has power over another. For us, the readers, it makes the person being nasty seem rather pathetic, even though the person on the receiving end is still having a bad time. Dickens lets us see how people with power over others are often pretty useless—people who in real life, if we were to come across them, we wouldn't take seriously. More often than not, he does this through the words they use, and the way they repeat themselves or repeat the style in which they speak. Dickens was one of the first to do this in novels (it had happened in plays before), and he helped pave the way for TV sitcoms with their catch phrases and punch lines.

Uncle Pumblechook's behavior makes Pip uncomfortable—yet

again, he feels less than he is. But off they go to Miss Havisham's house, "which was of old brick, and dismal, and had a great many iron bars to it. Some of the windows had been walled up; of those that remained, all the lower were rustily barred."

The girl who comes to meet them is forthright, if not rude. When

Pumblechook wonders if Miss Havisham might want to see him too, she cuts in with "Ah! But you see she don't." Pip observes that "She said it so finally and in such an undiscussible way" (*undiscussible* is another one of Dickens's own words, there to express deeply felt emotions and ideas). As they cross the courtyard together, Pip calls the girl "miss" and she calls him "boy," even though, as Pip tells us, they are about the same age. And the conversation is awkward. She has the upper hand and behaves like an unpleasant, bossy schoolteacher, one moment quizzing him, the next lecturing him, the next telling him what to do. Dickens lets us see what kind of person this girl is in quick strokes, all in her own words, as when she snaps at him, "But don't loiter, boy."

And then we are taken again into the realms of mystery and terror:

> We went into the house by a side door—the great front entrance had two chains across it outside—and the first thing I noticed was, that the passages were all dark, and that she had left a candle burning there. She took it up, and we went through more passages and up a staircase, and still it was all dark, and only the candle lighted us.

You'll remember that Pip was cleaned up to come here and that Mrs. Joe and Uncle Pumblechook told him he should be grateful: he was going to meet someone who must be looked up to and admired and thanked for taking him on. Instead, he is being led into the dark, into a place where it would be easy to get lost, somewhere that is scary. Is Dickens suggesting here, with another of those symbols, that climbing up the ladder of society is like this? That you may have to go where you will feel alone, uncomfortable, and scared? This is certainly what hits us next:

> At last we came to the door of a room, and she said, "Go in."
>
> I answered, more in shyness than politeness, "After you, miss."
>
> To this, she returned: "Don't be ridiculous, boy; I am not going in." And scornfully walked away, and—what was worse—took the candle with her.

Yes, things *are* getting worse. Here Pip is on the very brink of taking what might be the first step up the ladder, and he is alone, in the dark, and being told that he is "ridiculous." In his own words: "This was very uncomfortable, and I was half afraid."

Pip opens the door, and instead of being comforted, what he sees there makes him feel even worse. With some of the best word painting in all Dickens's writing, we look with Pip's eyes around the room. "No glimpse of daylight was to be seen in it." It's all lit with candles, and by telling us what furniture there is—a lady's dressing table—we realize that Pip is in the grand lady's bedroom, a place where someone who comes from near the bottom of the ladder, like Pip, should never be, unless as a servant. But as Pip says, she was "the strangest lady I have ever seen, or shall ever see."

She was dressed in rich materials—satins, and lace, and silks—all of white. Her shoes were white. And she had a long white veil dependent from her hair, and she had bridal flowers in her hair, but her hair was white. Some bright jewels sparkled on her neck and on her hands, and some other jewels lay sparkling on the table. Dresses, less splendid than the dress she wore, and half-packed trunks, were scattered about. She had not quite finished dressing, for she had but one shoe on—the other was on the table near her hand—her veil was but half arranged, her watch and chain were not put on, and some lace for her bosom lay with those trinkets, and with her handkerchief, and gloves, and some flowers, and a prayer-book, all confusedly heaped about the looking-glass.

It was not in the first moments that I saw all these things, though I saw more of them in the first moments than might be supposed. But, I saw that everything within my view which ought to be white, had been white long ago, and had lost its lustre, and was faded and yellow. I saw that the bride within the bridal dress had withered like the dress, and like the flowers, and had no brightness left but the brightness of her sunken eyes. I saw that the dress had been put upon the rounded figure of a young woman, and that the figure upon which it now hung loose, had shrunk to skin and bone. Once, I had been taken to see some ghastly waxwork at the Fair, representing I know not what impossible personage lying in state. Once, I had been taken to one of our old marsh churches to see a skeleton in the ashes of a rich dress, that had been dug out of a vault under the church pavement. Now, waxwork and skeleton seemed to have dark eyes that moved and looked at me. I should have cried out, if I could.

"Who is it?" said the lady at the table.

Imagine yourself coming across this scene, with your head full of escaped convicts trying to kill you, soldiers capturing convicts, a sister and uncle who boss you around and terrify you and make you feel small, and a girl who makes you uncomfortable.

In these two paragraphs, describing what Pip sees, Dickens actually writes in different ways. The first paragraph is almost entirely made up of what Pip sees. In the second, he takes us back and describes Pip's thoughts and how he was figuring things out then. Pip also begins to tell us what the place reminds him of. The writing goes deeper, from simply showing us what's there and what can be seen, to what Pip as narrator is feeling, how he works things out, and even how his past comes into play.

Once again, we might think about symbols. Miss Havisham is very rich and lives in a grand place, and yet she's all decaying, shrinking and dying. Is this what it's like at the top of the ladder? At this time in Britain, people were doing all they could to take power away from people at the top of the ladder, and working toward more people having the vote. Is Dickens saying that people at the top are decaying, useless, and, as we shall see, frozen in time?

Next, Miss Havisham makes Pip come close so that she can look at him. She tells him that she has got a broken heart and wants Pip to amuse her by playing in front of her. Pip can't or won't—or both—and mumbles apologies, hoping that it doesn't get him into trouble with Uncle Pumblechook and Mrs. Joe. The writing here is really good at showing the difference between the adult Pip, who is telling the story, and Pip the boy. This stops the storytelling from being simple: it gives us two Pips, two voices. It is as if Pip is swimming in a pool but also standing on the side watching himself at the same time! This double-voiced story-telling helps Dickens make us think about something we all do every day: we look back at things that have happened to us, relive them in our minds, and wonder what they meant. Should I or shouldn't I have behaved like that? Why did that person treat me like that? Dickens can be described as a moral writer, because he makes us wonder about the rights and wrongs of the way people behave; he's also a psychological writer, because he shows us how people do their thinking. Here are the two Pips:

> I . . . stood looking at Miss Havisham in what I supposed she took for a dogged manner.

This is Pip looking at himself swimming in a pool, as I've described it. And here he is speaking from the pool itself:

> "I am very sorry for you, and very sorry I can't play just now. If you complain of me I shall get into trouble with my sister, so I would do it if I could; but it's so new here, and so strange, and so fine—and melancholy—"

This double-voiced storytelling is perhaps one of the most important ways in which *Great Expectations* works on us, and we'll see it at its most powerful in just a minute.

In the next part of the scene, Miss Havisham orders the girl, Estella, to play with Pip. Estella says:

> "With this boy! Why, he is a common labouring-boy!"
>
> I thought I overheard Miss Havisham answer—only it seemed so unlikely—"Well? You can break his heart."

What an extraordinary moment! First of all, there is the naked snobbery of Estella, which, if we are on Pip's side in this story, we will feel is really nasty and wrong. Then, unbelievably, we hear Miss Havisham urge Estella on to an act of pure cruelty. Is this why she has asked Pip to come, so that he can have his heart broken? And is there some ganging up going on? Mrs. Joe looks up to Pumblechook, who looks up to Miss Havisham, who is intent on ruining Pip. There's certainly a sense of danger.

Well, Pip and Estella play cards, and the game is Beggar My Neighbour. Is this a joke in a book called *Great Expectations,* which is about going up the ladder? Do you have to make someone else a beggar to become rich? Quite likely, because the very next words we read come from Miss Havisham. "Beggar him," she says to Estella. Something sinister—even vicious—is in the air, an upper-class woman urging her stepdaughter to "beggar" a poor boy who has done no more than come and play for the woman's entertainment! But it's only a game—or is it?

While they play, Pip realizes why the room is like it is: "everything in the room had stopped, like the watch and the clock, a long time ago." But his thoughts are interrupted by Estella saying with disdain, "He calls the knaves, Jacks, this boy! . . . And what coarse hands he has! And what thick boots!"

In comes the adult Pip, the storyteller:

> I had never thought of being ashamed of my hands before; but I began to consider them a very indifferent pair. Her contempt was so strong, that it became infectious, and I caught it.

Here we see the older Pip realizing that this moment was a turning point in the younger Pip's life. He says he felt something he'd never felt before in his life (ashamed) and from then on he was different ("I began to"). And he's describing deep, deep feelings in the very heart of his being. The younger Pip is now ashamed of how he speaks, what he looks like, and who he is. Anyone who has ever felt even remotely like this knows that it's a very difficult position to be in. If you're not happy with who you are, how do you get through each day? Surely you'll have to change things: You can discover the good things about who you are and tell the people who make you ashamed to leave you alone. Or you can alter all the things about yourself that make you ashamed, and turn yourself into someone you're not ashamed of. What will Pip do? Judging by the older Pip's comment—"Her contempt was so strong, that it became infectious, and I caught it"—he is going to try the getting-rid-of-the-stuff-that-makes-you-ashamed route. Will he be able to, or does the old saying "A leopard can't change its spots" mean that he'll fail?

So Dickens gets us thinking. It's almost as if he goes beyond setting his characters a challenge. He sets *us* a challenge too: does your knowledge of how human beings behave match how *this* human being behaves?

It's clear that Dickens is no fool when it comes to how people think. Look once again at that sentence: "Her contempt was so strong, that it became infectious, and I caught it." Mostly when people look down on us, it makes us angry. But many of us also feel something quite subtle and, in its way, painful: we notice the contempt and it annoys us, but part of us becomes contemptuous of the very same thing. For example, someone might criticize your appearance. It makes you angry. You think that the person who said it isn't so great-looking either, but the next thing you know, you're looking in the mirror, thinking that the person who said it was right! You start to feel the same way about yourself as the person who said those horrible things. You've caught it, just like you might catch an illness.

Psychologists have all sorts of names for this. When people like Malcolm X and Julius Lester and other African American thinkers tried to work out why some black people seemed to accept what white racists said about them, they called it "internalizing the voice of the oppressor." Here Pip shows how when it came to class, he ended up doing just that—feeling the same way about himself as Estella did.

The rest of the chapter shows the older Pip reflecting on all the pain and humiliation he had felt at Miss Havisham's, as well as at the hand of Mrs. Joe. But the young Pip can't and won't free himself from the pain, because he is attracted to the very thing that is causing him the pain. He thinks Estella is beautiful, and he is starting to want her even as he wants not to be Pip, the "common labouring-boy."

We have come to one of those moments that happen in stories, films, and plays, where we want to say to the hero, "Don't do it. Don't go down that path." But of course, another part of us says, "Go down that path. I know it means ruin, but I want to see whether you'll be able to get yourself out of the mess."

There is no one better than Dickens at creating moments like this. They are, if you like, emotional cliffhangers, not simply a matter of wanting to know what happens next, but also of wanting to know what our hero will feel next, what he or she will think are the rights and wrongs of the matter. I reckon that if these moments seem to us complicated and full of difficult choices that we really care about, then we are looking at great writing. I think Dickens achieves exactly this, at this moment in *Great Expectations*. If you think so too, from what I've written here, you'll go and read the book. It's much better than simply reading the passages I've chosen and what I've been saying. It's like being taken on a journey that affects the whole of your being.

MR. PICKWICK

From THE PICKWICK PAPERS

CHAPTER FIVE

The Legacy

CHARLES Dickens became a celebrity. Wherever he went, people wanted to see and hear him. Whenever he wrote stories and articles, people wanted to read what he had to say. He was a success. Whether it made him happy or not is another matter.

Dickens died in 1870. If that seems an unbelievably long time ago, I'll just say to you that I was born in 1946. That means when I was a boy, I knew a few very old people who were children in the last year or so of Dickens's life. So what has happened to his books since then?

Dickens didn't live long enough to see the invention of moving film, animated film (cartoons), or television. But these kinds of entertainment have gobbled up his works and made hundreds of different shows for us based on his stories. Most people reading this have probably come across at least one of the following: Walt Disney's *Mickey's Christmas Carol* (1983), David Lean's film of *Great Expectations* (1946), or the musical *Oliver!* (first performed in 1963). There have been many, many TV adaptations of his novels as well, which have the advantage of following the pattern of Dickens's way of writing—in parts, separated by time. If they run for six or so episodes, they have the chance to get deep into the detail of the original books.

Some purists don't like these film and TV adaptations. They say that the books were written as books and should be read as books. Anything else is not worth looking at. I'm not in that camp. I think that we live in what is called an "inter-mediate" world. That is to say, we jump from one kind of media to another—from books, to the Internet, to newspapers, to TV, to movies. Nearly everything we read or watch is touched by something that comes to us in another media. When we go to see a film, we've often read reviews about it in the newspaper or seen interviews with the stars on the television. If we read a book, quite often we see something about it on TV, read a review of it in the paper, or see a film version of it first. Everything is commenting on everything else across all the different kinds of media.

So for me, Dickens lives in the inter-mediate world. I've seen him in the theater, in a cartoon, in a feature film, and many times on TV; I've read his books, I've read books about his books, and I've read hundreds of articles and reviews of his books. I've even read articles about the books about his books, and possibly articles about the articles about the books about the books! And as you read what I've written here, you're reading a book about his books too.

The Dickens that Dickens invented is in his books, but the moment those books came out, he became the Dickens other people invented by talking and writing about him or by making new versions of his stories. I hope that what you have read here will send you back to the Dickens that

MRS. GAMP

From MARTIN CHUZZLEWIT

Dickens invented, and that you'll find an interest and a pleasure there that will stay with you all your life. I also think it will make seeing all the other Dickenses, in film and on TV or video, even more enjoyable.

Charles Dickens has become part of our language. In most places in the English-speaking world, you can call someone a Scrooge and they'll know you're referring to the miser in *A Christmas Carol*. Many people will also know what you're talking about if you mention Oliver Twist asking for more. "More? Who do you think you are? Oliver Twist?" This means that Dickens invented something mythic or archetypal—a scene or a moment that speaks for millions of other moments in millions of other people's lives. We recognize it as representing something: the nerve of someone daring to challenge his or her superior; the gross and unfair way in which that superior might not let them have something. For a writer, creating one of these mythic moments is a fantastic achievement. It means that he or she has noticed something about how human beings deal with each other that really matters. Here are some other great Dickens phrases and sentences:

"If the law supposes that . . . the law is a ass—a idiot."

"Teach these boys and girls nothing but Facts. . . . Stick to Facts, sir!"

"Barkis is willin'."

"It was the best of times, it was the worst of times."

"Mr. Squeers . . . had but one eye, and the popular prejudice runs in favour of two."

As I've mentioned before, we even have the word *Dickensian*. My dictionary says it can be used to mean "squalid social or working conditions, like those described in Dickens's novels." Think of a cramped, old-fashioned, fusty place, with an old man there checking things off in an ancient book. It's a tribute to the fact that Dickens, more than anyone before or since, shows us what goes on in the minds of people who work in shops and offices.

It is also said that Dickens invented Christmas. The Christmases that are described in *A Christmas Carol* and his other books are occasions for eating, drinking, singing, and having a good time, no matter what difficulties or sadnesses come before and after. In writing them, Dickens took what was already happening in some places and gave it a mythic feel, so that people who read his books or saw his shows went away thinking, I would like to have a Christmas like that. He lived at a time when many people believed that having too much fun, especially on the birthday of Jesus Christ, was wrong, and there was a struggle between those who thought, Have a good time, and those who thought, Stay quiet, stay holy. The fact that Charles Dickens's view of Christmas seems to have won shows how deep into our whole way of life his writing has reached.

Key to Pages 88~89

The Pickwick Papers
24 Bob Sawyer
25 Samuel Pickwick
27 Tony Weller
28 Sam Weller
38 Alfred Jingle
39 Augustus Snodgrass
40 Dumkins
41 Luffey
42 Serjeant Buzfuz
43 Job Trotter
44 Mr. Justice Stareleigh
56 Joe the fat boy

Oliver Twist
29 The Artful Dodger
30 Fagin
35 Bill Sikes
36 Oliver Twist
37 Mr. Bumble

Nicholas Nickleby
3 Mrs. Squeers
22 Wackford Squeers
51 Newman Noggs

The Old Curiosity Shop
7 Nell's grandfather
8 Little Nell
9 Sampson Brass
10 Sally Brass
23 Mr. Chuckster
31 Daniel Quilp
32 Dick Swiveller
33 The Marchioness
47 Thomas Codlin
58 "Short" Harris

Martin Chuzzlewit
1 Mark Tapley
2 Mrs. Gamp

57 Seth Pecksniff

A Christmas Carol
18 Ebenezer Scrooge
52 Bob Cratchit
53 Tiny Tim

Dombey and Son
6 Captain Cuttle
21 Mrs. MacStinger
46 Paul Dombey

David Copperfield
4 Uriah Heep
5 Betsey Trotwood
15 Wilkins Micawber
19 Edward Murdstone
34 David Copperfield
59 Daniel Peggotty

Bleak House
14 Inspector Bucket

26 Jo the crossing sweeper
54 Mr. Chadband
55 Prince Turveydrop

Little Dorrit
12 Amy Dorrit

A Tale of Two Cities
50 Thérèse Defarge
60 Sydney Carton

Great Expectations
11 Abel Magwitch
13 Miss Havisham
16 Philip "Pip" Pirrip
17 Estella
48 Mrs. Joe Gargery
49 Joe Gargery

Our Mutual Friend
20 "Rogue" Riderhood
45 Silas Wegg

Timeline

Important dates in Dickens's life and significant events that occurred in literature and society

1811
- The census records 12 million people in the British Isles. About 2.5% of the adult population can vote.
- London is the largest city in Europe, with a population of more than a million.

1812
- **Charles John Huffam Dickens, son of Elizabeth and John, is born on February 7 in Portsmouth.**
- Great Britain and Napoleon Bonaparte's France are the two current major powers, at war with each other and other countries worldwide.

1813
- Jane Austen's *Pride and Prejudice* is published.

1814
- **John Dickens is posted to the London Navy Pay Office.**

1815
- The Corn Law, which fixes the price of grain and thereby drives up food prices, causes riots.
- The British defeat France at the Battle of Waterloo.

1817
- **John Dickens is posted to Chatham in Kent.**
- The stethoscope is invented.
- The end of public floggings for women convicted of crimes.

1818
- Mary Shelley's *Frankenstein* is published.

1819
- A crowd of 50,000 gathers in St. Peter's fields in Manchester to hear a speech on parliamentary reform. Local authorities panic; 11 are killed and 400 injured in what becomes known as the Peterloo Massacre.

1820
- The transatlantic slave trade taking Africans to the Americas reaches a peak.
- George III dies and is succeeded by the prince regent, George IV.

1821
- **Dickens starts at William Giles's school in Chatham.**

1822
- **The Dickens family moves to Camden Town, London.**

1823
- The Grimm fairy tales are published in England as *German Popular Stories*.

1824
- **Dickens starts work at Warren's Blacking Factory.**
- **John Dickens is arrested for debt and sent to Marshalsea prison.**

1825
- **Dickens is sent to London's Wellington House Academy.**
- The first public railway, built by George Stephenson, opens from Stockton to Darlington.

1827
- **Dickens starts work as a solicitor's clerk at Gray's Inn, London.**

1828
- The Duke of Wellington becomes prime minister.

1829
- **Dickens becomes a freelance reporter at the Doctors' Commons.**
- Sir Robert Peel founds London's Metropolitan Police.
- George Stephenson's locomotive the *Rocket* wins a speed contest, reaching 24 miles per hour.

1830
- George IV dies and is succeeded by William IV.
- Agricultural uprisings known as the Captain Swing riots occur all over England.

1831
- **Dickens works as a parliamentary reporter.**
- Newspapers not approved by the government are prosecuted.
- Michael Faraday discovers electromagnetic induction.
- A cholera epidemic sweeps England. Outbreaks also occur in 1848, 1853–54, and 1866.

1832
- The first Reform Act is passed. Voting is extended to the middle classes.

1833

"A Dinner at Poplar Walk" is published in the *Monthly Magazine*.

※

∽ Slavery is abolished in the British Empire.
∽ A Factory Act limits the working day of children under 12 to 9 hours. Those under 18 can work no more than 12 hours. Young children are allowed to leave work for 2 hours a day to attend school.

1834

∽ **Dickens becomes a reporter for the *Morning Chronicle*.**
∽ The Poor Law Amendment is passed, and parish workhouses are introduced.
∽ The Tolpuddle Martyrs are transported to Australia as punishment for trying to form a trade union.

1836

Sketches by Boz is published.

※

The Pickwick Papers is published monthly between **March 1836 and October 1837.**

※

∽ **Dickens marries Catherine Hogarth.**

1837

Oliver Twist is published monthly between **January 1837 and March 1839.**

※

∽ **Dickens's first child, Charles Culliford Boz, is born.**
∽ William IV dies and is succeeded by Queen Victoria.

∽ The Registration Act means that all births, marriages, and deaths must be registered.

1838

Nicholas Nickleby is published monthly between March 1838 and September 1839.

※

∽ **Dickens's second child, Mary, is born.**
∽ Regular Atlantic steamship service begins.

1839

∽ **Dickens's third child, Kate Macready, is born.**
∽ The bicycle is invented by Kirkpatrick Macmillan.
∽ William Fox Talbot announces his invention of photography.

1840

The Old Curiosity Shop is published weekly between **April 1840 and February 1841.**

※

∽ Sir Rowland Hill introduces the penny post.
∽ Samuel Morse invents the telegraph.

1841

Barnaby Rudge is published weekly between **February and November.**

※

∽ **Dickens's fourth child, Walter Landor, is born.**
∽ **Dickens tours Scotland.**
∽ England's Great Western Railway is completed.
∽ The Thomas Cook travel agency is started.

1842

∽ **Dickens tours America.**
∽ The employment in mines of women and children under 10 is outlawed.

1843

Martin Chuzzlewit is published monthly between **January 1843 and July 1844.**

※

A Christmas Carol is published in one volume in December.

※

1844

- Dickens's fifth child, Francis Jeffrey, is born.
- The Dickens family moves to Italy for an extended stay.

1845

- Dickens's sixth child, Alfred D'Orsay Tennyson, is born.

1846

Dombey and Son
is published monthly between October 1846 and April 1848.

- The Dickens family visits Switzerland and Paris.
- Edward Lear's *Book of Nonsense* is published.
- Hans Christian Andersen's stories are first published in English.
- The potato famine in Ireland sends hundreds of thousands of people to America.

1847

- Dickens's seventh child, Sydney Smith Haldimand, is born.
- Sir James Young Simpson, professor of midwifery at Edinburgh University, first uses chloroform in an operation.
- Charlotte Brontë's *Jane Eyre* and Emily Brontë's *Wuthering Heights* are published.
- The Ten Hours Act limits the working day of women and children.

1848

- Dickens's sister Fanny Burnett dies.
- Chartists march on London and deliver a petition with 6 million signatures to Parliament.
- Revolutions occur all over Europe.
- Karl Marx and Friederich Engels's *Communist Manifesto* is published.

1849

David Copperfield
is published monthly between May 1849 and November 1850.

- Dickens's eighth child, Henry Fielding, is born.
- The gold rush begins in California and Australia.

1850

- Dickens's ninth child, Dora Annie, is born.

1851

- Dora Annie and Dickens's father, John, die.
- The Great Exhibition is held in London's Hyde Park. More than 13,000 exhibits are viewed by more than 6 million visitors.
- Herman Melville's *Moby-Dick* is published.
- 23,000 Sunday schools across Britain offer free lessons to working-class children.
- The British census reveals that half the population lives in towns.

1852

Bleak House
is published monthly between March 1852 and September 1853.

- Dickens's tenth child, Edward Bulwer Lytton, is born.
- *Uncle Tom's Cabin*, by Harriet Beecher Stowe, is published.

1853

- Dickens tours Italy; he gives his first public reading of *A Christmas Carol* in Birmingham.
- Smallpox vaccination is made compulsory in England.

1854

Hard Times
is published weekly between April and August.

- The Crimean War begins.

1855

Little Dorrit
is published monthly between December 1855 and June 1857.

- Sir Joseph Bazalgette of the Metropolitian Board of Works submits a plan (completed in 1875) to create adequate sewers in London.

1856

- Dickens buys Gad's Hill Place on the outskirts of Rochester.

1857

- Dickens meets Ellen Ternan.
- Hans Christian Andersen visits Dickens—and outstays his welcome.
- Uprisings against the British East India Company begin.
- The use of hulk ships, anchored vessels holding prisoners awaiting transportation, comes to an end.
- The Matrimonial Causes Act permits men—but not women—to divorce on the grounds of adultery.

1858
∾ **Dickens separates from his wife.**
∾ During the so-called Great Stink of London, the smell of the Thames is so bad that a bill is rushed through to construct a massive sewer scheme.

∾ The British government takes over the rule of India.

1859

A Tale of Two Cities
is published weekly between April and November.

∾ Charles Darwin's *The Origin of the Species* is published.
∾ In America John Brown attempts to lead a revolt against slavery and is executed.

1860

Great Expectations
is published weekly between December 1860 and August 1861.

∾ Jean Lenoir makes a gasoline engine automobile.

1861
∾ The American Civil War begins.

1863
∾ **Dickens's mother, Elizabeth, and his son Walter die.**
∾ The first underground railway in London is completed.
∾ Charles Kingsley's *The Water Babies* is published.

1864

Our Mutual Friend
is published monthly between May 1864 and November 1865.

∾ A Factory Act makes unhealthy conditions in factories illegal.

1865
∾ **Dickens is involved in the Staplehurst railway crash and suffers permanent shock.**
∾ Elizabeth Garrett Anderson becomes Britain's first licensed female doctor.
∾ Abraham Lincoln is assassinated.
∾ Lewis Carroll's *Alice's Adventure in Wonderland* is published.

1866
∾ The first transatlantic submarine cable is completed, enabling telegraphs to be sent between Europe and America.

1867
∾ **Dickens tours America for the second time.**
∾ The Second Reform Act increases the British electorate.

1868
∾ **Dickens returns to England and tours.**
∾ The Trades Union Congress is founded.
∾ Louisa May Alcott's *Little Women* is published.

1869
∾ **Doctors order Dickens to discontinue his readings.**
∾ The Suez Canal is opened.

∾ Imprisonment for debt is abolished.

1870

The Mystery of Edwin Drood
is published monthly between April and September, but is unfinished.

∾ **Dickens gives his last public reading on March 15.**
∾ **Dickens dies on June 9.**
∾ Parliament passes the First Elementary Education Act, making school attendance until the age of 12 compulsory.